A

"Ever since Greg wrote a poem about my experiences as a child actor in Hollywood, I have been a fan of the Awesome Rev. His simple yet poignant verse has helped me articulate my faith in God and other people."

—Karolyn Grimes, Zuzu Bailey in *It's a Wonderful Life*

"With a poet's pen, Greg Asimakoupoulos is able to bring clarity and poignant observations to today's headlines. There are many commentators today, but Greg is the only person I know who can use the daily news to highlight moral truths in free verse. His voice is unique among us."

—U.S. Congressman Peter J. Roskam (IL-6)

"I find great delight recommending Greg's poetry. He is a close friend and constant encourager to the ministry of CBS. We always post his thought-provoking poetry on our website. I know you will be blessed by reading his creations."

—Camilla Seabolt, Executive Director of Community Bible Study

"The poetry in this volume conquers contemporary complexity with a mixture of rhapsodic prose and an almost eerie moral clarity. It projects buoyancy and hope while reflecting, with optical precision, the spontaneous surgings of the human spirit. Well done Reverend Greg!"

—Rabbi Daniel Lapin, American Alliance of Jews and Christians

"Greg Asimakoupoulos' whimsical way with words will take your mind on a poetic journey. But, you should be warned that his paradoxical pattern of playful words will most often have your mind pondering the pressing issues of our day."

— John G. Blumberg, national speaker and author of *Silent Alarm: A Parable of Hope for Busy Professionals*

"For more than two decades I have appreciated Greg Asimakoupoulos' creative way of stringing words together. The denomination I serve has been enriched by his unique contributions both in the pulpit and on paper."

—Glenn R. Palmberg, President of The Evangelical Covenant Church

"My long-time friend is a true raconteur. Greg freely takes whatever is offered up from the passing parade as fodder for poetic commentaries.His word pictures are at times deeply probing, deliberately ironic, or have a touch of the godly. The reader should expect the unexpected".

—David S. Noreen, Editor, seniorlifestyle.org

"There's no "rhyme or reason" why you would NOT want to grab this book! Pastor Greg is a gifted communicator with the ability to put into prose what you're thinking but cannot always articulate! His writings are contemporary, innovative poetry peeks into the heart of man — and God — in a world gone mad. Read him once and you'll be hooked — I am!"

—Peggie C. Bohanon, publisher of peggiesplace.com

Rhymes & Reasons

Rhymes & Reasons

by Greg Asimakoupoulos

Partial Observer Books
Lynchburg, Virginia

Published February 2008

The poems contained within Rhymes and Reasons originally appeared on The Partial Observer at partialobserver.com.

ISBN-13: 978-1-434-84185-8
ISBN-10: 1-434-84185-5

Cover illustration and book design by Mark D. Johnson
Author photo by Tony Vedrich

Partial Observer Books
www.partialobserver.com

This volume is dedicated to the four women in my life who allow me the time it takes to poetically reflect on the world and who regularly remind me how much they love me. Thank you Wendy, Kristin, Allison and Lauren Star.

CONTENTS

PEOPLE

WAR

HOLIDAYS

SPORTS

FOREWARD

For over four years the unique poetry of Greg Asimakoupoulos (pronounced "AWESOME-uh-COPE-uh-less") has graced the web pages of The Partial Observer, an online opinion journal. He has provided keen insight and commentary on the news of the day with both wit and artistry in a weekly column called "Rhymes and Reasons." His endlessly inventive wordplay provokes, in turn, both laughter and thought, touching on a wide array of topics, from our preoccupations with pop culture and sports to the horror of war and natural disasters. The constant thread that runs through it all, that shapes his outlook and informs his opinion, is Greg's Christian faith.

As a poetic commentator, Greg likens himself to a political cartoonist, often employing hyperbole to make his points. But while "Rhymes and Reasons" is typically written in reaction to current events, the poems collected in this volume have a certain timelessness that extends beyond the news that inspired them. At times, Greg draws upon his own experiences, as with "Leaving Home," written upon sending his daughter off to college. Who would not be moved at this eloquent snapshot of that bittersweet moment? His ability to capture, through poetry, what so many others have felt has caused many of these poems to spread like wildfire as readers eagerly pass them on to friends and family. His creative meditations on significant holidays, many of which are included here, are among the most popular pieces in The Partial Observer's seven-year history.

As well-suited as Greg's poems are for internet publication, it is particularly gratifying to see them in a printed collection, organized by category for the first time. This is an easy-to-read book that invites you to share it with others. We have received many Letters to the Editor and reprint requests in response to Greg's poems over the years, and it is always interesting to see how the various pieces resonate for various reasons with the Partial Observer's diverse audience. The politically-passionate will find something new to debate; baseball fans will see their game in a new light; and the faithful will find new inspiration.

Naturally, not everyone will agree with all of Greg's views, which makes The Partial Observer the perfect home for "Rhymes and Reasons." It is a place where opposing opinions are welcome and respected – where the point is not to shout to the world, but rather, to request a conversation. Whether you are new to Greg's poetry or a longtime reader, it's never too late to join the dialogue.

Mark D. Johnson
Founding Editor, partialobserver.com
January 2008

FAMILY

That Certain Someone

A father's love is a universal longing.

There is a certain someone I've longed for all my life.

Someone to watch me catch the ball.
Someone to help me when I fall.
Someone to say "I know you tried."
Someone to listen to my whys.
Someone to pay when I just can't.
Someone to see things from my slant.
Someone to hold me when I'm scared.
Someone to make sure I'm prepared.

Someone who loves me yet says "no"
and when I protest lets me go.
Someone who waits till I return
and then inquires "Whaddya learn?"
Someone who knows me totally
and overlooks the worst in me.
Someone who takes me at my word
and doesn't judge me as absurd.

Someone whose dealings are quite fair.
He arbitrates to clear the air.
Someone whose hugs aren't always earned.
He never hoards the things he's learned.
Someone whose friendship is for keeps.
He prays for me before he sleeps.
Someone whose patience won't run dry.
He aches with me each time I cry.

This certain someone has a name
and though he'll never dance with fame,

today I'm feeling mighty glad
that God gave me this one called dad.

Leaving Home

The hidden costs of college have little to do with tuition.

When your kid leaves home for college,
your emotions fall apart.
You can picture him in diapers.
You can see her tracing hearts.
You remember when he started
kindergarten, then first grade.
You could swear it was a week ago
she sold you lemonade.
There were Cub Scouts, ballet lessons,
Little League and soccer games.
There were sleepovers and campouts
roasting hot dogs on the flames.
There were Barbies, trucks and braces,
family trips to Disneyland.
It seems like only yesterday
you held that little hand.
Now that hand grasps a diploma
as that grown-up voice says "Bye…
I'll be home for sure Thanksgiving.
What's that leaking from your eye?"
It's a bittersweet occasion.
You're so proud this day has come.
But to see that empty bedroom
leaves you nauseous and half-numb.
It's a heartache felt by millions

who have watched their children leave.
When you let go of the ones you love
you cannot help but grieve.

A Tribute to a Lifelong Coach

Lessons my dad taught me.

Some say there is no perfect dad.
But they don't know the one I've had.
For more than fifty years this man
has modeled life for me.

Since I first joined the human race,
my father showed tough love and grace.
He knew I needed discipline
so coached me how to run.

But more than law and leniency,
my loving dad gave time to me.
Although he had a stressful job,
he sought me out at home.

When I was just a little tyke
he taught me how to ride a bike.
He made the time to throw the ball
and took great pride in me.

He kissed my cheek and hugged my neck
and very often wrote a check.
He helped me see that love can be
expressed in varied ways.

With that in mind my dad taught me
to treat my wife like royalty.
And so I learned to love my wife
the way he loves my mom.

He also showed me men can weep
and pray with kids before they sleep.
The cues he gave me as a kid
have helped me raise my girls.

My dad remains a proud Marine.
And while he's not as strong or lean
as when he fought back in the war,
he's taught me freedom's price.

And though my dad is growing old,
he still is prone to be quite bold.
He's quick to chide me when he thinks
I'm holding out on God.

He warns me not to work too much.
He offers tips on stocks and such.
He never fails to stop and pray
when he knows I'm confused.

But I don't mind. I trust his heart.
This one who's coached me from the start
will train me 'til the day he dies.
That's just what coaches do.

Paw Prints in My Heart

A final conversation with my dog the day that Kandi died.

As I look in your trusting eyes
to say my tearful last goodbyes,
I find it hard to let you go.
You're such a part of me.

The years we shared are now a blur
since you were but a ball of fur.
I still can see you in my mind
unleashed and running free.

But now you're sick and not yourself.
I grieve to know you've lost your health.
Yet you brought boundless joy to me.
I hope somehow you know.

And as I stroke your shiny coat,
a lump grows large within my throat.
I wonder if you understand
this really is farewell.

You look at me as if to say,
"Just stay with me. Don't go away."
And so I will, my little one,
as you lay down to sleep.

And though the time has come to part,
you've left your paw prints in my heart.
A heart that breaks imagining
my life when you are gone.

This poem is dedicated to the memory of Kandi Kisses Asimakoupoulos who passed away in the poet's arms on Wednesday, June 28, 2006 one week shy of her 15th birthday. It was written a couple hours before the mobile vet arrived to facilitate the necessary procedure.

Mother Knows Best

A tribute to the poet's mom who turned 80 this week.

Robert Young
starred on TV
before my mom was old.
He played a father who knew best.
At least that's what I'm told.

Those were the days
when dads were king.
Like Beaver Cleaver's dad
or Ozzie Nelson...
or Ben Cartwright...
Their sons were lucky lads.

But what about
The Beaver's mom?
Or Ricky's?
Hoss's too?
While dads are great,
there are some things
that only moms can do.

Like wipe your tears
when you fall down
and scrape your chubby knees
or say "God bless you" meaning it
each time you had to sneeze.

FAMILY

My mother
nursed me back to health
whenever I was sick.
She brought me juice
and comic books
and popsicles to lick.

She told me
that I was the best
when I was just okay.
But in her mind I really was
Her praises made my day.

She taught me
all about the Lord
and helped me understand
the pressures I would feel at school.
She helped me take a stand.

My mom has heart,
but also brains.
She helped me cram for tests.
And when I needed love advice,
it's true, my mom knew best.

When I left home
and took a wife
She felt somehow replaced.
I know that it was hard for her.
I saw it in her face.

But bless her heart,
in time she saw
she had no need to fear.
I needed both. A wife and mom.
She smiled from ear to ear.

She's one
creative grandmother.
My brother's kids
and mine
love spending time
at Nana's house
They think she's quite divine.

When Dad got sick
and nearly died,
my mother made me proud.
She mustered courage,
modeled faith
and prayed for him out loud.

As time went by
and she slowed down,
my mom refused to stop.
This fashion plate
can still turn heads
and loves to thrift store shop.

At eighty,
this one who gave me birth
embraces each new day.
She journals what she did
each night
before she hits the hay.

Her name is Star.
Uncommon, yes?
That's fine.
My mom's unique.
She sparkles like
the jewels she wears
while cuddled with her Greek.

And so this tribute
to the Star
I proudly
call my mom.
Keep twinkling
and light my night
until God brings
your dawn.

The Father of the Bride

Advice to Coach Holmgren from his pastor.

When you stand beside your daughter
and you hear the Wedding March,
I am guessing you'll feel something
like a sliver in your heart.

Though you're thrilled beyond description
that your baby's now a bride
you will have a strange sensation
like an itch deep down inside.

It's a bittersweetish splinter
that you cannot tweezer out
cause it's wedged and twisted sideways.
It's what good grief's all about.

It's a shard that's caused by memories
of those precious years you had
planting seeds of faith and wisdom
as her mentor, as her dad.

It's a sliver that you'll live with.
You'll thank God that it is there
for it's just one more reminder
what you've shared is really rare.

Adoption Has a Face

Celebrating the amazing story of an unwanted baby.

Adoption is special.
It serves a great need.
But not all adoptions work out.
Sometimes those adopted
are prisoners of sorts
imprisoned by questions and doubts.

"I do not belong here.
I'm not quite sure why.
I just know I feel so alone."
Though clothed, fed and sheltered,
Hugh longed to be loved.
He wanted much more than a home.

Like others adopted,
he pondered his past
imagining who gave him birth.
"How could she reject me?"
"Am I damaged goods?"
He struggled embracing his worth.
Unwanted, mistreated
quite tragic, and yet
Hugh's story was not fully told.
The Lord had a purpose

that would not be known
until the young boy had grown old.

A beauty named Norma
would capture his heart.
He'd marry and become a dad.
With four precious children
and one faithful mate,
he thanked God his life wasn't bad.

The wounds of his childhood
began to be healed.
The Father he'd longed for, he found.
A Savior, a Shepherd,
a mother-like Friend
had freed him from memories that bound.

Then Hugh found his calling.
He started to write.
This tall lanky lad had a gift.
He traveled, found stories,
kept journals of notes
and then through his research he'd sift.

The publishers loved him.
One book became two
and soon Hugh had found his career.
The boy once adopted
discovered his voice.
His purpose in life became clear.

"Each life is a novel
and needs to be told.
A story of joy, sweat and pain.
I want to write chapters

that help others see
how grace transforms losses to gains."

His life an example
of that very thing,
Hugh wrote countless books, but what's more.
The best one by far
is the last one he wrote.
It's a book you've been long hoping for.

It's a book about writing.
It's a primer of sorts.
It's the volume you need so you can
put pencil to paper and memories to print
for your children, the good, bad and grand.

** Hugh Steven's success as a writer is validated by the more than 30 books he has written as a missionary biographer with Wycliffe Bible Translators. His most recent book is actually a textbook for those who would like to write their own story. It is called "The Nature of Story and Creativity." In its pages, Hugh shares insights and suggestions for capturing your unique life experiences on paper to be enjoyed by your family, friends and colleagues and for the generations to come. "The Nature of Story and Creativity" can be ordered on Amazon.com.*

As you might have guessed, I know Hugh Steven personally. As a matter of fact, I married his oldest daughter twenty-five years ago.

Summertime at Grandma's House

Longing for the good old days and a great old lady.

As kids each summer we would go
to Grandma's house in Idaho.
In Nez Perce country near Lapwai
we had a five-star place to stay.

With cousins we'd play by the hour
within the barn where hay bales towered.
We'd ride the horses, milk the cows
and toss old corn cobs to the sows.

We all found shade on her front porch.
The summer sun could really scorch.
And side-by-side on Grandma's swing
we'd listen to the robins sing.

At night we heard the crickets chirp,
while watermelon we would slurp.
We'd fall bone-tired on our beds
and dream of how we'd soon be fed.

The frying bacon woke us up.
The fresh-squeezed orange juice filled our cups.
Her eggs and spuds adorned our plates.
First Grandma prayed and then we ate.

We kids ate much but she ate more.
Her height and width were 5 feet four.
But we weren't bothered by her weight.
It was good proof her food was great.

And there we'd sit when we were done.
Those table times were lots of fun.

Our Grandma spoke of childhood
back in the Blue Ridge Mountains wood.

She told us how she met "The Greek"
who coaxed a smile when he would speak.
His accent made his English fun.
And soon enough, her heart he'd won.

She'd arch her eyebrows and she'd wink
which caused us kids to sort of think
that maybe some of what she'd said
was bull that was baloney fed.

I miss those days at Grandma's place.
I miss her girth and godly face.
I miss how simple life was then.
I wish it was like that again.

Graduation Joys and Woes

Calculating the cost of a college education.

Just last week my firstborn daughter
(clad in tasseled cap and gown)
proudly clutched her college sheepskin
in a small Midwestern town.

I could see her back in preschool
as she walked across the stage.
But then when she turned and smiled,
my young princess came of age.

In my head I started adding
just how much her B.A. cost.
But those exponential numbers
avalanched and I got lost.

There is more than just tuition.
You've got books and room and board.
Then there's clothes and spring vacation
(and insurance for the Ford).

That diploma's worth a fortune.
So it makes sense (don't you think)
that my daughter's name be printed
with pure gold and not black ink?

Yes, I mined the bank but never
found the hidden Mother Lode.
It's the price a father pays while
traveling down the Parent Road.

You spend all that you've been saving
to invest in your kids' lives
and then pray they finish their degree
in four years not in five.

Still and all I can't help wonder
now that Kristin's finally through,
having majored in psychology
what can she really do?

Did I hear someone say grad school?
Are you kidding? Don't you know?
I have other bills that beckon
and have two more girls to go.

FAITH & CULTURE

God Remains our Source of Courage

A hymn of hope for days of despair.

God remains our source of courage
when we're traumatized by terror.
When we're haunted by the headlines
and the violence everywhere.
Hear God whisper in the silence
"Don't despair, I'm in control.
Hurting hearts and broken cities
will at last one day be whole."

God can feel the pain of suffering
when grenades and bombs explode.
When a son is robbed of living
at a checkpoint on a road.
Then God whispers in the silence
"Justice will in time be done.
I will stand with those who need me
'til my Kingdom fully comes."

God invites us to be trusting
when we find that faith is hard.
When we're fearful for our safety
and our nerves are frayed or jarred.
Still God whispers in the silence
"Even when your faith is weak,
I will keep your feet from stumbling
when your way is dark and bleak."

A God-less Pledge? God Forbid!

An appeal to the High Court to leave the Lord alone.

If not "under God," then whom are we under?
If He's not in charge, then who is? I wonder.
A phrase on our money declares Whom we trust.
Is it just a slogan corroded with rust?
Though now it is lawful to sing Irving's song,
will "God Bless America" soon be deemed wrong?
Yet are we one nation except under Him?
To make such a claim is an ungrounded whim.
Because all our framers were mindful of God,
to absent Him fully is treasonous fraud.
The woman who raises a torch in her hand
stands ready to welcome the world to our land.
But God is not welcome. There's no room, it seems,
for Him who gave rise to America's dream.
How dare we be God-less. How foolish indeed,
when He is the reason our nation was freed.
The Pledge without God's name is best left unsaid.
To say it without Him suggests He is dead.
And so I'm appealing to those gowned in black
that our Pledge of Allegiance be maintained intact.

A Temporary Ceasefire

The 'under God' face-off is far from over.

The battle over "under God"
has ceased for now you see
and all because the dad who sued
did not have custody.
It seems instead of ruling on

the merits of the case,
the Justices in Washington
found loopholes in the lace.

So even though God didn’t get
His rightful day in court,
He can for now still be esteemed
by students tall and short.

This war of words is far from done.
That phrase may yet be shot.
But until then acknowledge God
and pledge with all you’ve got.

Marriage by the Book

Why gay marriage is an oxymoron.

When the Lord created marriage,
it was clear He had a plan.
He designed a lifetime union
'tween a woman and a man.
He intended they'd have children.
That is why their bodies fit.
And this opposite attraction
was the world's survival kit.
Married man and married woman
is a universal norm,
though the ceremonies vary
as do licenses and forms.
Just ask Webster, he will tell you.
Marriage means a groom and bride.
That's inherent in its meaning.

There is nothing else implied.
It assumes that men and women
(anatomically distinct)
pledge commitment to be faithful
with a kiss and pen and ink.
Marriage is a holy calling.
It's a contract of two lives.
It's a legal binding promise
made by husbands and their wives.
It's a bond God sees as sacred.
It's a covenant of love.
It's a metaphor of Oneness
like the Trinity above.

America's New Civil War

How the gay agenda stands to divide our nation.

It's not the Union and the South,
but it's a Civil War.
As same-sex unions meet the law,
I'm dreading what's in store.

Like Roe v. Wade, what's right's at risk.
The battle lines are drawn.
What's normal is now up for grabs
and so the fight is on.

The rights of gays will not be left
behind in this campaign.
They'll be debated long and loud
as candidates take aim.

Our nation will be ripped in two.
The death toll may be high.
If gays and lesbians win out,
the truth is what will die.

St. Arbucks is a Sacred Place

America's favorite coffee spot offers a religious experience

It's communion... of another kind
where caffeine seekers can unwind
to drink in the sweet ambiance
that St. Arbucks provides.

As congregants both young and old,
we're seated close and thus are bold
to talk of life (latte in hand)
and taste the mystery.

We lift the cup and share our lives
in honest words that aren't contrived.
And if inclined, we all confess
our failures and our dreams.

St. Arbucks is a sacred place
where those who run the human's race
can sip the nectar of the gods
awake to what is good.
It is quite sanctuary-like
where mothers and their little tykes
can find a refuge from routines
while seated near the fire.

There are no stained glass windows there
but those behind the "pulpit" care
about the thirst we long to quench
and "preach" through what they pour.

What Cheers was thirty years ago
is now St. Arbucks. Don't you know?
A church where we are known by name
and feel like family.

Beware of the Spiderless Web

Exposing the dangers of internet porn.

Curves and angles
bodies tangled
just a click away.
Your heart beats faster,
but disaster
stalks you like a prey.

Air-brushed vixens
lure you to them
with their lustful eyes.
And though they're phony,
men real lonely
stare and fantasize.

Cyber sex sites
twist your insides
like a hurricane.
Be sure they'll duly

(and quite cruelly)
flood your life with shame.

Don't live guilty
feeling filthy.
Break the cycle quick.
Though you may seem fine,
you've become blind
to what makes you sick.

If you're peeping
you are keeping
wrongful company,
for those you're Googling
will start ruling you
just wait and see.

Or better yet, don't.
Say, "Lord, I won't
ever look again.
And through Him you can
be a new man
unconcerned with skin.

Cracking the Code

Exposing the true secret about Jesus.

The Church has kept a secret
two thousand years or so.
It has the truth that's been withheld
from those who need to know.

But unlike Dan Brown's fiction
that claims Christ had a son,
the secret that has not been shared
is that He is "The One."

The one who is our Savior.
The only way to God.
The one who died and then was raised,
though some call him a fraud.

And still the doubters wonder
if He can cleanse their guilt.
But when they're asked to spill the beans,
most Christians start to wilt.

And so this truth stays hidden
from millions in the dark
who are quite clueless of St. John,
of Matthew, Luke and Mark.

It's time the code was broken.
This secret must be told.
If Jesus is the only way,
His people must be bold.

So don't boycott the movie.
It's good you have a look.

Unless, of course, you've made a point
of reading Dan Brown's book.

Me thinks The Code's a blessing.
Can you remember when
so many skeptics pondered Christ?
Let dialogs begin.

Goodness, Gracious, it's St. Tenacious

Meet the patron saint of all who persevere.

Ignatius is a saint who's loved
as is John of the Cross.
Teresa is the choice of some,
but her prayers leave me lost.

Tenacious is my patron saint,
not Ambrose or Bernhard.
He didn't flinch, dropout or run
when trusting God got hard.

He persevered and got back up
when critics put him down.
And though at times the Lord seemed deaf,
he prayed without a frown.

Tenacious didn't buy the lie
that says ease is our right.
Instead he found that faith grows best
within the soul's dark night.
Tenacious planned on having days
at sixes and at sevens.

"Because," he said, "we're still on earth.
Perfection's found in Heaven."

I love this saint and yet it seems
he's often overlooked.
You'd be hard-pressed to find his stuff
in Desert Fathers books.

And yet Tenacious speaks to those
who listen to his heart.
Tenacious Christians stay the course.
They finish what they start.

The Deceiving Beauty of Autumn Leaves

Examining the death of morality in progress.

They dangle most delectably
like Eden's apple did.
But neath their orange and reddish hues,
a tragic truth is hid.

The autumn leaves cling to the tree,
but soon each one will fall.
Misleading beauty caused by death
invites us to recall

such colors can seduce our thoughts.
Their beauty is a lie.

They "wow" us with what looks like life
but they themselves have died.

Morality is withering.
God's standards (slighted) fall.
Our brittle culture (veined by lust)
chants "tolerance is all!"

Indecency in media
is rampant. Porn prevails.
With church attendance in decline,
what flourished once now fails.

The tree is growing naked fast.
Unclothed, ungodly, stark.
The chill of winter can be felt
as brilliance becomes dark.

In God They Trusted

The Declaration of Dependence Our Presidents Have Voiced.

We honor former Presidents
who steered our Ship of State.
In powdered wig or blow-dried hair,
each made our nation great.

Each took an oath acknowledging
a Higher Power's aid.
And in an office oval-shaped,
each squared his knees and prayed.

Each understood America's
uniquely servant role
in planting freedom's seeds abroad
no matter what the toll.

Those living and those long-since dead
found strength in one short phrase.
"In God We Trust" was grounds for hope
on good (and stressful) days.

And so we think of George and Abe,
of Gerald, Jimmy, Bill
and all the others in the list
who sought God for His will.

What It Takes to Make Love

A recipe for commitment Jessica and Nick overlooked.

A virgin bride
put faith aside
to be seduced by fame.
For young Ms. Simpson
marriage was
a made-for-TV game.

A Saintless Nick
with abs of brick
paved Jessica's success.
But while they played
celebrity
their marriage was a mess.

The Newlyweds
claimed skill in bed,
but making love is more
than what takes place

between the sheets.
The way you really score

is saying no
when work says go
and leave your spouse for weeks.
It's staying true
when one night stands
are what your passion seeks.

You score big time
when you unwind
and hold each other close
to watch the news
or share your dreams
while sipping hot Red Rose.

True love is made
when feelings fade
and beauty bows to age.
It's made when you
live out "I do"
and pay commitment's wage.

Love's recipe
it seems to me
requires more than thyme.
It's time well spent
with just a hint
of more of yours than mine.

Love Lessons from the Pitts

What we can learn from Jennifer and Brad's break-up.

The nation's sad
that Jen and Brad
have opted now to split.
The spotlight of celebrity
has left them in the pits.

They seemed so right
with matching height
each with a chiseled bod.
And since they'd made it for four years,
their breakup now seems odd.

But in a town
where up means down,
the ones who do survive
have found it takes hard work and will
to make a marriage thrive.

The secret to
what keeps love true
is saying it's for keeps.
It's talking much and listening more
and knowing when to weep.

It's giving in
and in and in
when you know you are wrong.
It's making up and getting down
while dancing to your song.

It's being blind
when time's unkind
to your mate's sagging frame.

It's holding hands and taking walks
and playing table games.

It's staying in
when lustful whims
might tempt you to bail out.
By choosing to remain in love
you give your vows their clout.

A Sure Cure for Stress

Post-op advice for Bill Clinton.

When you're pooped, uptight and frazzled
and your plagued by anxiousness,
there's a simple diagnosis.
You are suffering from stress.

You are taxed by unmet deadlines.
You are driven by demands.
You're a mess of frayed emotions
like some stretch-out rubber bands.

It's a low-grade chronic sickness
that will leave you nearly dead,
if you don't address the symptoms.
First of all, go straight to bed.

When you wake up, eat your breakfast.
Spend some time with God in prayer.

Let the Lord review your date book.
Offer up your angst and cares.

Take a walk or jog three miles.
Don't neglect your exercise.
Watch your diet. Drink much water.
Boycott burgers, Cokes and fries.

Make the most of meals with family.
Share your feelings. Make amends.
View each day as priceless treasure.
Count your blessings. Laugh with friends.

Learn the art of saying "Sorry!
While I'd love to I just can't."
Try to just say no more often.
Let it be your freedom chant.

Guard your day-off like a soldier
wearing sneakers, jeans and cap.
Let yourself enjoy a hobby.
Every Sunday take a nap.

Even though it's not a cancer,
stress can kill you just the same.
So determine you will fight it.
Make a stress-free life your aim.

Graze Anatomy

Not all appetites are created equal.

Metabolisms
are unique.
So it's not fair
to say I sneak.

Three squares a day.
Who says?
Not me.
I have a graze anatomy.

I have this need
to snack and munch
by 10 or so
and after lunch.

And then come 3
or maybe 4,
I have the urge
to eat some more.

But do not think
I've lost control
I only eat till
I feel full.

My meals are many
but they're small.
And so I don't
gain weight at all.

So please don't judge
my feeding craze.
While some pig out,
like cows I graze.

PEOPLE

The Circle is Complete

A Tribute to Johnny Cash.

I'm feeling kinda poor today.
The Cash is finally gone.
That pocked-face man who dressed in black
has sung his final song.
He sang about a love gone bad,
about a life ill-spent.
His songs conveyed the pain he felt
as down sin's road he went.
But when the man in black met Christ,
his whole demeanor changed.
Although he still could sing the blues,
his heart was not estranged.
He walked the line (and sometimes tripped).
Like us he stumbled on.
But with his sweetheart by his side,
a weak man became strong.
In May his June found wings and flew
to Canaan's happy land.
And Johnny died a bit back then.
She was his one-man band.
The two at last are one again.
The circle is complete.
Their hands are raised in grateful praise
because of Jesus' feat.

Beyond the Myths of Camelot and Mayberry

How JFK's tragic death changed our view of reality.

Our memories are in black and white
as we recall that silent night
when we ate supper without words
the day our leader died.

We cried when Walter Cronkite said
that JFK was really dead
and that our dreams of Camelot
were only make-believe.

A son's salute. A horse-drawn hearse.
Our kingdom went from grief to worse
as Vietnam and racial war
gave way to riot gear.

What's clear amid the blur of facts
is how a rifle (like an axe)
would separate the world we knew
from what it would become.

Our naïve nation came of age
as protests, free love, pot and rage
would prove our moral bankruptcy,
yet free us to be real.

For forty years we've grieved a loss
that catapulted us across
a chasm that had frightened us
from leaving Pleasantville.

Beyond the myth of Mayberry
we've seen what Opie couldn't see...
that life ain't fixed in half an hour,
but God is always there.

The Long Goodbye

Our mourning for Mr. Reagan didn't begin this week.

Ten years ago,
removing a cloak of suspicion,
Ron donned a vest of vulnerability
and admitted what many had feared.

The rumored vandalism was true.
Without invitation or welcome,
Mr. Alzheimer's disease had broken into his mind
and begun to rob Mr. Reagan
of that brilliant sense of reason, wit and recall
we all had come to love.

Back then we began our goodbyes.
It was as if Nancy's Ronnie
had mounted one of his much-loved horses
and slowly rode beyond his ability to hear us.
So we waved so long
and mused how short
eight decades of life really is
(and how cruel it can be sometimes).

Out of sight (and out of mind),
it seemed our 40th President left us then.
But he hadn't really.
His slow private ride into a mind-blinding sunset
provided us plenty of time to make peace with
what has become the dreadful destination of too many.

And so it seems appropriate that we would mourn
a good long time this week.
It seems only right that his corpse be carried
from one coast to the other and then back again.
This one for whom America was truly beautiful

had to go from sea to shining sea one last time
before his pastor could pronounce
"ashes to ashes, dust to dust."
It was a must.
After all, the boy from the Midwest
left his mark in the west and the east
and not least of all in our hearts.

Filled with heads of state who respected him
and tales of a great leader who proved himself,
the National Cathedral is an appropriate sanctuary
to honor God and acknowledge a man of humble origins
known for both his patriotism and faith.

The church perched high above the city of monuments
is the perfect place to memorialize a leader
too many (sadly) took for granted.
And so a House of God
not far from what was once his House of White
shelters his flag-draped earthly dwelling
while a grateful grieving nation watches.

But we would do well to remember
it is his earthly dwelling only.
While we are left to contemplate our own
forthcoming journey through Death's Valley,
the man we mourn is quite alive
and at long last
clothed in his right mind.

A Super Man Nonetheless

Remembering the resilient Christopher Reeve.

We pause to grieve
because Chris Reeve
just lost his earthly life.
This super man
had countless fans
and one heroic wife.
Courageously
Chris let us see
he WAS a man of steel.
Though paralyzed
he realized
what matters most is will.
And though confined
he never whined
about his tragic plight.
He learned to cope
while boasting hope
that day would follow night.
But with the dawn
we learned he'd gone
unlike the way he'd planned.
His dream to walk
by death was blocked.
Still Chris WAS Superman.

Memories of a Faded Rose

Remembering the life and legacy of Rosa Parks.

She wouldn't budge when on a bus
a white man said "My seat!"
She bravely sat and stood her ground
like wind-blown Kansas wheat.

It was a bus ride that began
a journey not yet done.
A trip toward equality
where blacks and whites are one.

No, a Rosa by any other name
would not smell as sweet.
Her very name was
the fragrance of freedom
to many a little girl (and boy)
who grew up in the contaminated
soil of the South
with hopes of a better life
and dreams of being as courageous
as Ms. Parks.
No, Rosa was not your garden-variety
kind of woman.
She was a rare specimen.
Though her life was marked by thorns
that stemmed from ugly prejudice,
Rosa bloomed with beauty.
Her solitary act of defiance
became a delightful bouquet of justice.

And as her shriveled lifeless frame
is laid to rest today,
may memories of this faded rose
inspire us I pray.

Barney of Mayberry

Taking time to cry for one who made us laugh.

Andy's tailor alters his only suit
transforming it from a wedding one
to one befitting a funeral.

Gomer's pile of discarded Kleenex
grows more mountain-like
by the moment.

It's all because Barney's fife
remains in its case
having sounded its last note.

The community band
of trumpets and tubas,
of clarinets and flutes
will never seem the same.

Yes, Mayberry's loveable deputy
has turned in his badge for good.
The carefree tar-heel town
is jailed by sorrow today.

Aunt Bea and Otis
and Goober and Floyd
are searching in vain for the key.

It's no wonder
Mayberry's resident whistler is silent.
Even Opie's at a loss for words.
But then, so are the rest of us.

Those big bulging eyes
and high piercing voice

won our innocent hearts
in a much simpler time.

But that was then
and now is now.

The death of Don knots our guts.
It lumps our throats.
The one who made us laugh so loud
now causes us to cry.

Peace to your memory, Barn.

The King is Dead

Remembering Johnny Carson.

We said farewell twelve years ago.
And now we say goodbye.
We missed you, Johnny.
Now we grieve. You were too young to die.

You were our late-night talk show king.
We loved you on your throne.
We paid you homage with our laughs.
For thirty years we groaned.

With Ed McMahon at your side
and Doc leading the band,
you ruled the night with wit and charm.
Your shows were never bland.

While trumpet fanfares are the norm
to welcome queens and kings,
"Heeeere's Johnny!" brought you out each night
from waiting in the wings.

There's no one who can take your place.
King Carson, you've no peers.
You've left a hole within our hearts.
Our cheeks are stained with tears.

Graham's Last Stand

Paying Homage to the Prince of Preachers.

Though quite feeble, Billy battled
to proclaim God's truth again.
He's as brittle as a cracker,
still this Graham has strength within.

He's resilient and determined.
Doctors shake their heads in awe
at this white-haired prince of preachers
who has led the world to God.

Once again he's home at Montreat
after preaching one last time.
This globe-trotting 'good news' spokesman
still can make the Scriptures rhyme.

He can still shape moral conscience.
And he will though he retires.
Billy's full-on bold commitment
is amazing. It inspires.

It's a kind of God-allegiance
too few Christians tend to pledge
in a culture of convenience
where our risks are often hedged.

May our Father bless our brother
as he faces what's to come.
Pray that Bill will keep on running
'til his race on earth is done.

Requiem to a Rebel Forever Young

Remembering James Dean on the 50th anniversary of his death.

East of Eden, north of Indy
James Dean headed west.
But it wasn't long
before his dreams came up short
and things went south.

His fast-paced lifestyle
stole his smile (and his tomorrows)
as the reckless speed at which he lived
became the reckless speed
from which he died.

For this baby-faced
rebel without a cause,
a fleeting taste of adulthood
was swallowed up in death.

Fairmount's fair-haired native son
had won the fame for which he'd longed
only to lose the chance to enjoy it.

No wonder America wept
as this bright falling star
(who burned out prematurely)
was swept from celebrity's stage.

And although Central Indiana
is left with the right
to claim the final resting place,
it's a somber privilege at best.

Even though James grew up a Quaker,
he seemed at odds with his Maker
when he cashed it all in
as he crashed.

It's likely James Dean once knew
what it meant to be Friends with God,
but God only knows
if (through faith) they embraced
the day that he died...
forever young.

Remembering a Valiant Queen

A eulogy to Coretta Scott King

The King's grand wife has left her throne.
Queen Coretta has gone home.
And in her passing North and South
with reverence grieve as one.

With quiet grace young Martin's mate
survived a heartache birthed by hate.

And we her subjects weep for one
who valiantly kept on.

I have a dream (and so do you)
that what she longed for will come true.
When prejudice and power plays
are exiled, judged and damned.

But until then "God save the Queen"
who kept alive her husband's dream
and taught us how to turn a cheek
while letting justice roll.

A Farewell to Falwell

Remembering a religious icon.

The Moral Majority all agree.
Jerry Falwell did well
but died too soon.
His fruitful life will continue to speak
though his silenced lips cannot.

From Thomas Road to Liberty,
this Baptist preacher helped us see
how true devotion to a cause
can reap big dividends.

He grew a church and college too
and then before Jim Bakker knew,
this Lynchburg televangelist
would rescue PTL.

His right-wing stance left some irate.
Sometimes his judgments (like his weight)
seemed way too heavy and unsafe.
He could be arrogant.

But far more good than ill was done
to help Christ's Kingdom fully come.
He had his faults, but don't we all.
In stumbling, he fell well.

The right has lost an advocate
who could be quite articulate.
But our entire country grieves.
A patriot has died.

"Hello, Americans! This is Paul Harvey!"

A poetic tribute to my childhood hero.

"Hello, Americans!" he's wont to say.
I hear him say it everyday.

His lilting voice conveys the news
while finding ways to spin his views.
Just hearing him, makes me feel warm
when icy headlines make me mourn.

Since I was just a school age lad,
I've heard him take what's really sad
and find a hook to help us cope
through God and country, dreams and hope.

His bumper snickers make me laugh.
His stories have a second half.
His sponsors are like family,
like Hillsdale, Bose, Hi-Health, page three.

My favorite newsman is unique
in what he says and how he speaks.
I think you'd call him my mainstay.
His name is Paul ...Harvey... Good day!

**Recently, while on vacation in Phoenix, I unexpectedly encountered Mr. Harvey taking his daily afternoon walk near the Biltmore Hotel. I greeted with a hearty "Hello, American!" He smiled and invited me to join him on his 1 1/2 mile stroll. For thirty minutes I savored a dream come true. Making the most of the fleeting moments, I asked the 88 year old newsman questions about which I've wondered since I first heard him on the radio when I was a boy of twelve. It was the highlight of my vacation.*

The Tenor of Our Grief

A Tribute to Luciano Pavarotti.

The phantom of the opera
holds a mask that hides his tears
A trio has become a sad duet.
The big man with the giant voice
who taught the world to sing
is silent. Pavarotti now is dead.

Those lyrics few could stomach,
Luciano brought to life.
Like a circus clown,
his singing coaxed a smile.
Opera music gained a hearing.
Like a rock star he found fame
though his weight and marriage failures
proved a trial.

Luciano, how we loved you.
No one else can take your place.
May you find in death God's mercy
on your soul.
With a voice that tempted angels,
you brought Heaven down to earth.
Now it's time to sing God's praises
loud and full.

The Time is Right

Bob Barker's well-deserved retirement comes with a price.

Five decades back
(ask Senor Wences),
Bob hosted Truth
or Consequences.

And even then
(his hair much darker)
we loved to watch
Roberto Barker.

As game show barker
he was best.
So Monty Hall
and all the rest

could not compete
or make a deal
the way The Price Is Right king
wheeled.

Bob bid contestants
"Come on down!"
while standing up
for basset hounds.

A dapper dresser,
Bob looked nice
while coaxing folks
to name their price.

From home I loved
to play along,
though most the time
my bid was wrong.

Still as I watched
The Price is Right,
my daily grind
seemed less uptight.

Bob Barker's presence
on TV
recalled the good old days
for me.

But now those days
have come and gone.
The game show barker
isn't on.

And so I pray
God gives him grace
as Bob prepares
for Life's Showcase.

Farewell to Dan Fogelberg

Mourning the band director's son.

The leader of the band we knew
was Dan's dear aging dad.
But wow, could his son write and sing.
A brilliant gift he had.

Much, much too soon young Fogelberg
has bid us all goodbye.
And like his lyrics bout his dad,
his death has made us cry.

At fifty-six he barely lived.
We can't help but miss Dan.
I only wish his time with us
had been ... well ... longer than.

Remembering Princess Di and Mother T

Calculating the wages of fame (and faith) a decade later.

August 31st.
The paparazzi's thirst.
The people's princess
raced for freedom.
Tunnel vision won.

A decade has gone by
since Lady Spencer died.
Still Will and Harry
(and their father)
grieve as no one knows.

And lessons yet remain
for those beset by fame.
The rich and famous
are the diet
of a hungry press.

Yes, fame can be a blight.
It robs you of your rights.
And renders you
a well-dressed prisoner
wishing you were free.

Unearthing Mother Teresa

And now a decade later
they're unearthing Mother T.
Some say the sainted nun was less
than she appeared to be.

They say her reservoir of faith
was leaky... filled with holes.
That she confessed to what is called
the dark night of the soul.

But those who doubt her virtue
do not fully understand
that doubting fertilizes faith
as only questions can.

The saints of old were not immune
from times when God seemed mute.
Their badge of faith was inner angst,
an ash heap and some soot.

What's telling about Mother T
is how she carried on.
In spite of doubt she didn't quit
until her life was done.

WAR

Pondering a Presidential Visit

Questioning another's motives reveals something about ours.

Hardly anyone knew
when the President flew
to Iraq back on Thanksgiving Day.
Though his top-secret trip
gave our soldiers a lift,
his detractors insist he will pay.
Was his mission of joy
a political ploy
just to shore up his sagging appeal?
Or was it a case
of a man touched by grace
who imagined how lonely troops feel?
I'll be first to confess
that it's easy to guess
what his motive for serving might be.
For it's when I'm not sure
that ones motives are pure,
it's because I assume they're like me.

The Naked Truth

An intimate look at war and sin.

Stripped of clothes and dignity,
naked prisoners on TV
demonstrate how war disrobes
the mind of what it good.

What we see before our eyes
shouldn't be a big surprise.

Those at war who seek revenge
will do most anything.

Add to that what lurks within
every person born in sin.
We are all quite capable
of doing shameful things.

Sin makes monsters of us all.
War's a bloody beast-like brawl.
Thanks to both, what's wrong seems right
and that's the naked truth.

Finally Home

Grieving for our fallen soldiers.

Your son waved goodbye
then left for Iraq.
You checked off the days
'til your boy would be back.

With pride in your heart
and fear in your face,
you spoke of your son
and a longed-for embrace.

And then...

He came back in a box
lifeless and still.
Home from a war
that wasn't his will.

Home to a nation
weary and worn.
Tired of being
divided and torn.

Home to a country
jaded and numb
that numbers the reasons
why peace can't be won.

Finally home on a
permanent leave.
His sacrifice questioned.
No wonder you grieve.

Back to the Future

What the ancient practice of beheading points to.

In the days of John the Baptist
cruel tyrants filled with hate
would decapitate their captives
serving up their heads on plates.

Fueled by rage and heartless motives
captors used the guillotine
as they executed "justice"
raining red on fields of green.

In Iraq they're still beheading
those they kidnap, torture, maim.
Without thought of humane treatment,
swords and daggers are a game.

Those who do such are the headless.
Mindless monsters, brainless beasts.
These with masks who wield their weapons
are the lowest of the least.

In a world inclined toward evil
what has been will always be
'til the Prince the Baptist promised
ushers in eternity.

A Day at the Beach

Remembering D-Day six decades later.

Forget for a moment
the price of gas
and contemplate a war long passed.
Consider the cost
for a day at the beach
that turned the tide toward peace.

The 6th month
The 6th day
60 years ago
11,000 airplanes
5,000 ships
150,000 troops
(mostly men less than 20 years old
carrying 80 pounds of equipment
toward a destination 200 yards through the sand)
10,000 casualties
4,000 dead

Millions abroad hoping
Millions at home praying
that the moustached-monster in Berlin
would finally meet his match.

11 months and 2 days later
those hopes were realized
and those prayers were answered.
But not without a hefty price tag.
The bottom line was more than a thin red one.
The cost was incalculable.

The Wanted One is Found

The irony of Saddam's capture at Christmastime.

The bearded man has now been shaved.
Not Santa Claus, but one depraved
whose evil bent and heartless greed
made Seuss's Grinch look nice.

This one who lived in luxury
was humbled (as we all could see)
when he who lived it up as king
was found down in a hole.

Unlike our King who left his throne
to make our sinful world his home,
Iraqi's ruler (now a slave)
did not lay down his rights.

The irony of Christmastime
is only lost on those quite blind

who cannot see the paradox
of wealth-to-poverty.

Within a farmhouse Christ was found
by common shepherds all around
who searched to find whom they believed
to be the Wanted One.

The search is over for the man
(the one called Jesus not Saddam)
who can alone bring peace to earth
and with it peace with God.

Adding Up What Divides Us

Why keeping score of the war isn't easy

It's been THREE years.
TOO long some say.
ONE wonders FOR what cause.
A FIVE star general in D.C.
admits to fatal flaws.

In war the numbers don't add up.
The totals are much more
than those who've died
and dollars spent.
There's all the bloody gore.

But don't forget
what's been achieved
as freedom spreads its wings.

Iraqi women, kids and men
have heard their future sing.

Counting the Cost

Looking for meaning in the mounting toll of war.

In this grim war
a hundred score
have come back in a box.
And still they die
while some ask "why?"
"Is Bush's brain but rocks?"

Two thousand troops
in funeral suits
with eyes forever closed.
Some say they died
for one man's pride.
Perhaps. But just suppose

they shed their blood
in Baghdad's mud
for those who nightly dream
of freedom's prize
and joyful sighs.
Do you know what I mean?

Although the toll
deflates my soul
and renders me so sad,
I still am for

this horrid war
that aims to curb the bad.

Iraqis need
(aren't we agreed?)
the chance to fend off terror.
They want our aid.
They're glad we've stayed.
Of course they want us there.

Endless War on Center Stage

The drama in the Middle East continues.

The Middle East's
on center stage
and in the West
we watch in rage.
The curtain's drawn
on what's become
a record-breaking run.

The Playbill
in our trembling hands
explains the plot
that plagues The Land.
A land God promised long ago
to Jacob's dozen sons.

The actors change
but not their roles
as scripted mayhem
takes its toll.

WAR

This drama titled Endless War
has far too many acts.

The theatre
(like those of war)
has no soft seats,
no walls or floor.
Its sets and props are Eden-old
and blood-soaked from their use.

An intermission
is quite rare.
And when it comes
we hardly care.
For once the air has cleared of smoke
the play begins again.

O God, please end
this show's long run.
It's time your stage play
Kingdom Come
is acted out
much like in Heaven
when peace will take a bow.

HOLIDAYS

NEW YEAR'S DAY

A New Year's Prayer

A month by month glimpse ahead.

In January as I think
of Dr. King's sweet dreams,
I pray that peace and brotherhood
won't ravel at the seams.

Come February when I see
young couples that I know,
please use me as a Valentine
to help their love to grow.

And then in March when old St. Patrick's
faith is called to mind,
arouse my will that I might serve
the homeless, bruised and blind.

In April when the rains of spring
awaken winter's sleep,
please let the truth of Eastertime
to help my faith go deep.

When May recalls the men that died
in bloody wars long past,
assure that what they fought to win
will somehow live and last.

In June when school is ended
and vacations have begun
convince me that I need a break,
some leisure and some fun.

And come July when on the Fourth
I praise my Uncle Sam,
please prompt me Lord to give you praise
for living in this land.

When August comes and hurricanes
start threat'ning folks down south,
don't let me gripe about small stuff
or get down in the mouth.

And in September when I get
to rest on Labor Day,
remind me that my work's a gift.
I'd hate to always play.

In dark October when your paintbrush
brightens dying leaves,
please move my heart with wonder
as they dance upon the breeze.

And then in bleak November
when I feast with family,
receive my thanks for all the ways
you prove your love for me.

And in December when I string
the lights and feel you near,
accept my gift of love, dear God,
for what you've done all year.

MARTIN LUTHER KING'S BIRTHDAY

Following the Doctor's Orders

Why Dr. King's prescription for racial inequality needs to be acted on.

I think we've really come quite far
since Doctor MLK, JR
prescribed a medication
for our nation's skin disease.

What Martin clearly diagnosed
reflects how quickly bias grows
when prejudice is overlooked
or countenanced as right.

The good Doc's remedy was clear.
We start by looking in the mirror
and taking stock of how we tend
to justify our hate.

And then he said to exercise
(not with our legs but with our eyes)
by being blind to color
as we look at those God made.

But then the doctor left us quick.
He died when we were still quite sick.
And yet in the past forty years
we're on the road to health.

Our skin disease is clearing up.
We're drinking from a common cup.
And as we swallow pride,
we taste our true equality.

VALENTINE'S DAY

Valentine Advice

What's at the heart of love's favorite day.

The hallmark of this holiday
is not a card with which you say
some mushy sort of sentiment
that seems contrived or canned.

It's sharing memories of the past
while eating slow or walking fast.
It's silencing your selfish wants
to hear the other's heart.

It's taking time and finding ways
to be a friend and offer praise.
It's holding hands or folding them
to thank the Lord for love.

A Walk to Remember

Looking at Valentine's Day through the lens of a lifetime.

Forget your dancing shoes.
Remember your walking stick.

Romance is a dance of passion
choreographed by the capricious emotions
of desire.

But lasting love is a daily walk
where the talk of commitment
makes steady progress
toward the destination of a lifetime.

It's an adventure trek into tomorrow
where the surprises you encounter
beyond the bend
are both a shared and priceless prize.

It's a hike on a mountain path
that encompasses breathtaking vistas,
valleys of disappointment
and fog-shrouded plateaus
where companionship
doubles your joy
and divides your sorrow.

It's a slow-motion shuffle
when, as an elderly couple,
you hold hands
(having held true to your word)
and whisper to each other,
"After all these years I still do!"

It's a lonely stroll
down a quiet corridor
that leads you to a certain room
where one connected to monitors and tubes
still recognizes your voice
and smiles as you ask
"Will you be my valentine?"

Don't settle for the fleeting dance of romance.
Make your relationship a walk to remember.

Not Your Ordinary Day

What's really at the heart of St. Valentine's Day.

It's a day for a card,
maybe roses and candy,
an upscale-ish dinner
with candles and brandy.

It's a day for conveying
what's deep in your heart
while holding hands walking
alone in the park.

It's a day for renewing
those wedding day vows
when, asking God's blessing,
before Him you bowed.

It's a day to remember
a Saint from the past
whose selfless devotion
beyond daily mass

resulted in prison
and scars on his back
as children who loved him
slipped notes through the slats.

It's a day you can ponder
you're God's valentine.
Both chosen and cherished,
He thinks you're divine.

GOOD FRIDAY

Good Friday Now and Then

Looking at the past through the lens of the present.

The calendar above my desk
announces that today is a good Friday.

But the headlines of my morning paper
counter that claim.
A river of crimson blood
flows through the parched dirt streets
of an ancient city.

It's a pity really.
Innocent life snuffed out.
Victimized by fanatic fundamentalists.
Warring factions who fashion a wardrobe of power
cloaking the city in a sinister fog.

"Bag dad and bury him,"
a jaded widow doubled in grief
chides her frightened children.
"Hurry please, before your father is disposed
upon some garbage heap."

This mother's mourning
continues late into the night.

"I rock my babies to sleep
wishing them sweet dreams
all the while praying my own will come true.
Dreams that my sons and daughters will be able
to grow up without being blown up
never to wake again."

The complaint of the ancient psalmist is voiced anew.
"Where is God anyway?"
"Why has He forsaken the helpless anyhow?"

The mother of Jesus knew a similar sorrow.
Hunched at the foot of a Roman cross,
Mary inched back in fear and revulsion.
Her swollen eyes looked through
tear-stained fingers at a lifeless body.
It was a body she knew only too well.

This dead man was once the baby
she had gently rocked to sleep.
This bloody corpse had once been the toddler
whose bloodied knees she had tenderly bandaged.
This object of her grief had (not so long ago)
been her twelve-year-old Bar Mitzvah boy.
You know.
The one who went missing for three days
only to eventually to be found in the Temple
talking with the elders.

And now that life
(which God had supernaturally given her)
was gone.

As she lived her own nightmare that day,
I doubt Mary dared to dream
she would again find her Son in three days time.

The injustice was just too blinding.
The pain too intense.
The reasons why the blood was flowing
not nearly clear enough.

Two women (separated by two millennia)
drank bitter dregs from a common cup.
One lost an Iraqi husband.
The other a Jewish son.
For neither was it a good Friday.
It was a bad news day all the way.

And in the midst of human agony
the likes of which few of us could possibly imagine,
God has a way of showing up unannounced *and unexpected.*
It's called Easter.

The Bar Mitzvah boy did it again!

EASTER

Don't Let the Grinch Steal Easter

Resisting the lie that says Easter's a hoax.

The Grinch, that green menace, is at it again.
As Easter approaches, just look at his grin.
It's broad and it's toothy and signals his plan
to tempt all the children, each woman and man.

If he has his way on this Grand Sunday morn,
they all will think chocolate is why they were born.
And then after breakfast, for eggs they will search
instead of deciding to dress up for church.

That emerald old tempter, so shrewd and so bold,
is heartless, deceptive, conniving and cold.

"Forget about worship," he protests. "How dull!"
Just eat Peeps and candy until you are full.
Don't bother with Jesus. Just go out to eat.
The sermon is boring. The songs all repeat.

"The story is spooky. There're corpses and caves
and an unlikely outcome for gullible knaves.
A dead man now living? How totally un.
When death scores a victory, the Grim Reaper's won.
There aren't second chances. Once dead, you are dead.
All empty-tomb claimants have rocks in their heads."

Oh really, Green Monster? You think it's a ruse?
Don't bad mouth a mystery that's really Good News.
You see, Mr. Grinch, when you're dealing with God,
you can't just dismiss what's unlikely and odd.

The fact you can't splain it does not mean it's fake.
I'd guess you are silenced by joy at a wake.
But that doesn't mean what you see is a fraud.
The grievers are joyful because they know God.

They know they will see their dead loved one again
and all because Jesus, once killed for our sin,
reversed the magnetic-like pull of the grave
as proof that his passion has power to save.

To save us from acting like we're in control
of our self-centered, self-righteous arrogant souls.
To save us from guilt and regret's residue
that deadens our faith-buds like bad rabbit stew.

To save us from lusting for status and money
and greed that breeds faster than prolific bunnies.
To save us from those who insist there's no room
in a logical world for a lone empty tomb.

Just look all around you. The earth that was dead
has left winter's casket. It's thriving instead.

Me thinks, Mr. Grinch, there's a parable here.
In old Mother Nature, it's perfectly clear
that what the church preaches each Easter as fact
is not just a story. True life MUST come back.

Observe earth's cathedral. Go on, take a peek.
A grand celebration awaits those who seek.
The tulips are trumpets. Hear budding trees sing.
Be still for the preacher. His name? Well, it's spring.

So in this fresh season when new life is seen,
beware of the tempter who's furry and green.
Don't let him convince you that Easter's 'bout eggs
or buffets of ham steak and little sheep's legs.

Instead, buck the culture and alter your search.
Try hunting for Jesus. Spend Easter at church.

EARTH DAY

Praying for a Sick Mother

Earth Day Reflections on Global Warming.

Mother Earth has got a fever.
Some insist it's no big deal.
Others say it could be fatal.
Doomsday prophets start to kneel.

Diagnosis? Global warming.
There are sweat beads on her brow.
She is having trouble breathing.
Just how much will God allow?

Major surgery is needed
Cutting out some things we do.
Like the fossil fuels we guzzle.
Going green may see her through.

We should pray that she'll recover.
After all, she is our mom.
May our Father who's in Heaven
intervene before she's gone.

MEMORIAL DAY

Don't Take Memorial Day for Granted

Granite headstones deserve to be decorated.

They called it Decoration Day.
A chance each year to humbly say
how much we owe to those now gone
who blazed our freedom trail.

It is a day to leave our homes
and journey to a yard of bones
where those who served sleep six feet down
awaiting Gabriel's horn.

It's there we'll place a plant or wreath
and think of those who lay beneath.

We'll thank the Lord for what they did
to benefit our lives.

In cemeteries far and near
we'll say a prayer and shed a tear
and count the cost of liberty
they paid on our behalf.

We'll also grieve for moms and dads
recalling special times we had.
And we'll resolve to spend less time
at work and more at home.

It is a somber holiday
which calls for more than rest and play.
It is for taking stock
of bonds that made us rich.

A New Haunt for Old Heroes

The greatest generation finally gets their just desserts.

The World War II Memorial
at last is finally done.
It calls to mind all those who fought
that freedom might be won.

Between the throne of Abraham
and George's monument,
the green-wreathed markers represent
the red blood that was spent.

They speak of battles long since waged
on foreign lands and seas
where adolescents came of age
while fighting on their knees.

Those posts of limestone fence the past
and block out needless noise.
In silence grandpas contemplate
the fears they felt as boys.

This ground is holy, temple-like.
It speaks of sacrifice.
It whispers "Peace must be maintained
no matter what the price."

And so with walkers, canes and limps
old veterans make their way
to reminisce, regroup and count
the cost they had to pay.

They say a prayer and wipe their tears.
Though stooped, they stand up tall.
Within a park that honors them,
they're heroes one and all.

Most holy God, I pray for these
now old and weak and tired.
Remind them that our nation's strong
by what they have inspired.

And for those who have long since died,
we think of them today.
May what they modeled live in us
as we clear freedom's way.

FOURTH OF JULY

From Sea to Shining Sea

A fourth of July salute to America the beautiful.

From Alaska to Nebraska,
from the tundra to the corn,
I'm amazed with wide-eyed wonder
at this land where I was born.

From the Blue Ridge to the Rockies,
from the East to way out West,
I'm convinced with every mile
that America's the best.

From the Islands to the deserts,
from the seashore to the sand,
I'm aware of God's creation
oceans blue and canyons grand.

From Atlantic to Pacific,
from the right to the left coast,
I am constantly reminded
why Americans can boast.

From the Bayou to the Boundaries,
from the South to points up North,
we've good cause to wave Old Glory
as we celebrate The Fourth.

Listening to Freedom's Cry

Something to ponder this 4th of July.

The birth cry of Freedom
heard so loudly at first
from a baby delivered in pain
can't be heard by deaf ears
in a nation at risk
that ignores those first sounds
to its shame.

What once moved us with passion
in decades long past
doesn't grip us the way that it did.
Seems our hearts rarely race
while saluting the flag
like when pledging allegiance
as kids.

And the right to assemble,
to worship and vote
has become commonplace in our minds.
To the fact that we're privileged
to do what we do
we're clueless
and too often blind.

We all take wealth for granted.
We think we're still poor.
We forget that most all of the earth
tends to struggle with basics
to just stay alive
while we minimize
what we are worth.

It seems we have forgotten
the 4th of July
isn't just an excuse to have fun.
In addition to hot dogs
and cold Mac and Jacks
on the lake in the warm
summer sun,

we have good cause to gather
with family and friends
and thank God for the land of the free,
for all veterans who served
to assure us the right
to both practice
and prize liberty.

For the numberless options
and chances to choose
where to live, what to eat and to wear,
for the laws that protect us
from what is corrupt
and that shield us
from what isn't fair.

For the peace on our home front
and allies abroad
and for soldiers who willingly fight
against forces of terror
with suicide bombs
who are dead-set
against human rights.

Let us thank God for Freedom
birthed so long ago
and the labor preceding her cry.

Let us ask Him to help us
again hear her voice
amid fireworks
in the night sky.

LABOR DAY

A Toast for Labor Day

Saluting the American workforce.

I lift my glass to those who work
the cabbie, waitress, soda jerk,
the gardener and the janitor
and mini-mart cashier.

I'm grateful for attorneys, too,
protecting us from those who sue.
And don't forget our family docs
and nurses they employ.

And then there are the brave who teach
and those at church ordained to preach.
The farmers, too, deserve our praise
plus salesmen on the road.

The firefighters and police
and car mechanics smeared with grease
help keep us safe and on the road
though often they're unsung.

This toast is also for our troops
who labor 'til their eyelids droop
defending freedoms we embrace
while taking aim at terror.

So here's to all who earn a wage.
This weekend they deserve the stage.
Because of them, our stress of life
is drastically reduced.

A Labor Day Tribute to the All-Night Worker

Saying thanks to graveyard shift survivors.

You punch the clock while others sleep.
That graveyard shift is long and deep.
At times it's like you're six feet down,
bone tired, feeling dead.

It's hard to go to bed at dawn
or after you have mown the lawn.
It really is unnatural
to sleep the day away.

You wake for dinner and you say
"I wish my job was in the day
for then I could have nights at home
and watch my favorite shows."

Still you're the envy of those damned
by traffic that is always jammed.
Those daytime workers only dream
of such a quick commute.

And truth be told the work you do
is valuable. Your boss needs you.
The overnights that you put in
mean far more than you know.

VETERANS DAY

A Tribute to an Unknown Soldier

Veterans Day reflections on the price of freedom.

Hey soldier,
even though I never knew you,
I want to thank you.

You loved our country just like I.
You bled red, white and blue.
You didn't run when Uncle Sam said
"Young man, I need you!"

The things you fought for
are the possessions I cherish.
They are privileges
I could never afford on my own.
Freedom from fear.
Freedom from want.
Freedom of speech
and freedom to worship God.

A treasure chest of priceless gifts.
That's what you bequeathed to me.

Because of you (and others like you),
I am wealthier than I can fully comprehend.
Still, in the end, in the pursuit of justice
(in which you gave your life),
it doesn't seem fair at all.

Why should you be called to give up
some of those freedoms
in order to make all of them possible
for those who are sometimes hesitant
to show their gratitude?

Hey soldier,
even though I never knew you,
I want to thank you.

I cried the day I heard you died.
As your flag-covered casket
was carried in slow-motion precision
to a waiting hearse,
my heavy heart grieved
with sighs too deep for words.

Hey soldier,
even though I never knew you,
God knew you intimately.
What is more He loved you.
He gave His Son to die for you.
And I'm praying that this loving God
will overwhelm your loved ones
with His comfort and compassion
as He under girds them

with His grace and peace.
After all, thanks to you I have
the freedom to publicly declare
my dependence on Him.

Hey soldier,
I'm grieving you're gone,
but I'm grateful for what you gave.
And even though I never knew you,
I just wanted to say thanks.

In Praise of Unpaid Heroes

Recognizing the worth of America's veterans.

I know a wrinkled balding man
who proudly served his Uncle Sam
and claims he'd do it all again
to fight for liberty

I think you've seen this man before.
This one who risked his life in war
and then returned without a limb
but with no real regrets.

He has a tale he's known to tell
of what it's like surviving Hell
and how it feels when buddies die
or lose their sanity.

Although he's brave, he's also shy
and tries to dodge the public's eye.
He's quite content to quietly
reflect on freedom's price.

But when he sees the flag go by,
this man is not ashamed to cry.
He stands up straight and then salutes
a banner he esteems.

I know that man and so do you.
He's rarely paid what he is due.
His name is VETERAN and he's earned
a place in history.

The Old Veteran

Celebrating the courage of those who continue to fight.

I know an old veteran
in my neighborhood
who lives in his house all alone.
Though he's dressed like a pauper,
you'd think him a king
most deserving a crown and a throne.

He sits in his wheelchair
remembering tanks
in which he once sat years ago.
His memory may falter,
but he still recalls
the details of war we don't know.

He thinks of those battles
when fear won the day
and grown men (like boys) wept for mom.
Those foxhole conversions
and frontline assaults
made him pray that he'd live to see dawn.

And he did, although wounded.
The soldier came home.
But sadly he'd not walk again.
His Uncle Sam called him
a hero most brave.
A nephew he proudly called kin.

The veteran then married
the love of his life
who cherished her soldier as gold.
They couldn't have children,
but never complained
convinced that as one they'd grow old.

But cancer thought different
and came in-between.
At sixty, his wife passed away.
And two decades later,
he still battles grief.
The old veteran fights sadness each day.

His uniform's faded
but hangs neatly pressed
near the wedding gown Sally once wore.
Two closeted symbols
of promises made
at an altar and frontlines of war.

I love that old veteran.
I call him my friend.
His courage convicts me to fight.
When I'm feeling defeated
or lost in the dark,
I just look down my street and see light.

THANKSGIVING

Don't Let the Grinch Steal Thanksgiving

Why genuine gratitude begins with contentment.

In Whoville the Grinch was quite greedy and mean.
The envy within him caused him to turn green.
Ungrateful and jealous, this monster-like grouch
spent Thanksgiving morning curled up on the couch.
No holiday baking. No holiday fun.
The number of chairs at his table was one.

It seemed that his appetite wasn't for food.
He always was stuck in the stuff-buying mood.
"Why cook up a turkey?" He said to himself.
"I'd rather add stuff to what's stuffed on my shelf."

The stores were all closed for the Great Day of Thanks.
But that was no problem. The green prince of pranks
could shop by computer to his heart's content.
And clicking his mouse, the Grinch spent and he spent.

The Great Day of Thanking went by really quick
and by spending and buying the Grinch got real sick.
But nobody knew it. And nobody cared.
For Grinches are selfish and Grinches don't share.
And if you are wondering the point of this rhyme,
then keep reading on past the end of this line.

In the -ville we inhabit there isn't a Grinch.
But sometimes we act just like him cause we're rich.
We buy what we want without batting an eye.
We silence our kids' "gotta-haves" when they cry.
We love to go shopping and spend major cash
while throwing away what's still good with the trash.

We envy our neighbor's new car and new boat
and find ourselves lusting to have her mink coat.
We want a new kitchen. New drapes would be fine.
And oh don't we love how our hardwood floors shine?

We long for the latest. We crave what is new.
We're not satisfied having one. We need two.
Two big screen TV sets. Two Lexus. Two homes.
There's two spouses working to service the loans.

And though when we're cut we bleed red not Grinch-green,
our selfish Grinch tendencies still can be seen.
Our hearts are thing-centered. They aren't good at thanks.
They start to beat stronger at Best Buy and banks.

It's hard to be grateful when there's more to buy.
We can't track our assets. In truth, we don't try.
Instead we're inclined to add up what we need.
First this and then that and then... Look at our greed!

And even on this day when turkey is king
we aren't satisfied with a leg and a wing.
We need mashed potatoes. We need candied yams.
We need beans and biscuits plus two kinds of jams.
There's tossed greens and Jell-o and cranberries too.
At least we are grateful we know how to chew.

But gratitude's not way high up on our list.
We feel so entitled it tends to get missed.
But that is not all we ungrateful folk do.
There's something that turns us a Grinch-greenish hue.
We rarely if ever say "I'm satisfied."
And if we did say it, we most likely we lied.

If we are forever fixated on more,
we can't be contented. Contentment's a chore.
Contentment is foreign. Contentment ain't fun.
And why should we settle when our dreams aren't done?

Why settle indeed? Because deep in our soul
we feel something's missing. It feels like a hole.
It's really a hunger that's long been ignored
by Grinch-like behavior that's caused us to hoard.

But, hey, it's Thanksgiving. The hungry are filled.
Let thirsts, dreams and longings be quenched met & stilled.
No turkey is needed. A ham will not do.
The feelings you long for hide deep within you.

Start counting your blessings. Look back, not ahead.
Be done being selfish. Be grateful instead.
Be grateful for fingers, for eyelids that close.
Be grateful that you can still smell with your nose.
Be grateful for legs that allow you to walk.
Give thanks that the tongue in your mouth lets you talk.

Give thanks for your children. Give thanks for your spouse.
Give thanks for your over-stuffed "imperfect" house.
Be done with Grinch yearnings. Let thanks fill your heart.
Acknowledge God's goodness. That's where it will start.

A Call for Pilgrim-like Praise

Why confession of ingratitude is an appropriate appetizer to this year's dinner.

They didn't land within our town.
They moored at Plymouth Rock.
Those ones who taught us to give thanks
trapped turkeys, deer and fox.

The Pilgrims feasted off the land
as new friends showed them how.
Their learning curve was steep and hard
without an ox-drawn plow.

And yet they didn't grouse and gripe.
With buckled-hats removed,
they knelt each night with praise to God.
His faithfulness they'd proved.

So many years have long since passed.
Our lives are far less stressed.
And yet it seems we aren't as quick
to claim how much we're blessed.

We feel entitled way too much
and lack the Pilgrim's flair
for recognizing all they had
with humble hearts and prayer.

So this year on Thanksgiving Day
let's honestly admit
what undeserving folks we are
in light of what we get.

With Thanks for Thanksgiving

What makes this holiday my favorite.

A feathered beast. A family feast.
Some football and some pie.
Thanksgiving is MY holiday
and here are reasons why.

It is the day I'm free to pray
at church OR City Hall.
The need to show God gratitude
seems natural to all.

My wife's great food. My brother's brood.
And time to just relax.
This priceless day is one fine gift
my Uncle Sam can't tax.

A lazy walk around the block.
A nap when I feel tired.
A game of Scrabble (Skipbo too)
and popcorn by the fire.

Simplicity (it seems to me)
describes this holiday.
No gifts to buy (or to return).
No customs to obey.

This day of thanks with beans and franks
would still be just as great.
What makes Thanksgiving what I love
is more than what I ate.

CHRISTMAS

The Night Before Christmas

Contemplating Christ's nativity and global conflict.

On this night before Christmas
those car bombs still blast.
The peace the Prince promised
is not coming fast.

There's bloodshed in Baghdad.
There's hate in Ukraine.
The conflicts in Israel
seem never to wane.

In bleak North Korea
a madman's in charge,
while deep within Africa
tensions loom large.

And in our own nation
the deficit's deep.
A blanket of terror
keeps millions from sleep.

The jobless and homeless
can't sing Silent Night.
They're hopeless and joyless.
Their prospects aren't bright.

We churn for our children,
afraid what's in store.
With gangs, drugs and violence,
they have their own war.

Emmanuel's birthday
is shrouded by fear.
It seems we've forgotten
that He is still near.

For though it appears
that at times there's no God
and all of this holiday hoopla's
a fraud,

the truth of this season
can't just be dismissed.
The message of Christmas
says we're on God's list.

He feels what we're feeling.
He grieves when we grieve.
He won't leave us lonely
on this Christmas Eve.

The best gift He offers
is peace in our hearts.
And when we unwrap that
the world peace thing starts.

A Politically-Correct Holiday is a Humbug

One jaded Christian's Christmas wish.

It's Christmas, but (for what it's worth)
what's grounded in the Savior's birth

is buried neath a holiday
politically correct.

The teachers call it Winter Break.
That makes me mad. For goodness sake,
two billion people in our world
are followers of Christ.

It seems to me a bit absurd.
We sing of Santa's flying herd,
but when it comes to caroling
it is a silent night.

I'm warned about the way I greet
the ones this month I chance to meet.
To wish them "Merry Christmas" is
considered quite uncouth.

Those life-sizes creches on the square
have been outlawed. It's so unfair.
The First Amendment guarantees
my right to celebrate.

Good Lord, these changes make me sick.
What once was yours is now St. Nick's.
The meaning of the virgin's child
is hardly understood.

If only I could help folks see
just what this season's meant to be.
Then maybe, Lord, the world would know
the peace you came to give.

O Little Town of Where-We-Live

A musical prayer of confession.

O little town of Where-We-Live
you surely know the score.
We give to those who give to us
and overlook the poor.
The homeless and the widows
don't have much Christmas cheer.
How can they when they live without
the basics through the year?

But we who live with all we need
take all of it in stride.
The holidays are good to us.
We rarely are denied.
We bake our Christmas cookies
and gather with our friends.
A concert here, a party there
and then the season ends.

But somehow something's missing
in spite of what we do.
If honest, we're quite empty
and joys it seems are few.
We end each year resolving
to break with old routines
and yet come next December
we're like we've always been.

This Christmas may God give us eyes
to see what makes Him cry.
And hearts to feel the pain he knows
when plans for justice die.

As shepherds left their livestock
we're called to leave our flock
to seek the place where Christ is found
uptown or down the block.

* *These lyrics can be sung to the tune of O Little Town of Bethlehem*

The Conundrum of Christmas Carols

How can we sing when the world is weeping?
In memory of the tsunami victims of 2004.

From silent night to deafening roar
as waves of terror washed ashore.
The product of a monstrous quake
left countless lifeless in its wake.
I heard the bells on Christmas Day
but soon those soft sounds went away.
Instead I heard loud screams of fear
that all around the globe could hear.
O little town of Bethlehem,
please weep for those who've lost their lambs
for once you knew such wordless grief
when death prowled like a heartless thief.
Joy to the World seems out of place.
Our planet's stunned and tries to brace
for untold sorrow still to come
as graves are filled in one by one.
Georg Friderik Handel's Comfort Ye
makes better sense to you and me.

It is a lyric forged in pain
in which Emmanuel speaks our name.
O Come, O Come Emmanuel
be near to those who feel like Hell
has found its way to where they live.
Give hope as only You can give.

I'm Dreaming of a Right Christmas

Examining the injustice of religious tolerance.

I'm dreaming of a right Christmas
when those who love the left
will hate the freedoms then allowed
of which I'm now bereft.
Like seeing live nativities
lit up on city squares
or saying "Merry Christmas, sir"
without it seeming rare.
Like hearing carols at the mall
instead of "winter songs."
Why is it Frosty rates so high?
Is Silent Night so wrong?
It's bad that I can't find Good Yule
on Hallmark greeting cards
while Hanukkah and Kwanzaa ones
are there. It's so bizarre.
The Christians' fest is pot-shot prone
chalked up to tolerance.
Yet other faiths are bullet-proof.
I think that's kinda nuts.

The liberty to practice faith
is guaranteed to most.
But if it's thought you're born-again,
you might as well be toast.
And so I dream of Christmases
that won't be a nightmare.
A day when what the law allows
is true for freedom's heirs.

Christmas.com

A look at the meaning of the Incarnation through the windows of technology.

Long ago in a land far away
an illegal operation was performed
and the human hard drive crashed.
Upon rebooting,
a garden variety virus was detected.
Lacking any means of self-repair,
mankind with mice in hand
clicked in vain.
But the Creator would not let
the unique technology
He'd designed remain inoperative.
Gazing through the windows
of eternity future,
He wrote a software program
He labeled "grace."
Although it was the perfect antidote
for the virus of sin,
this program had to be downloaded

before its benefits would take effect.
Proof that the download
had been successfully achieved
was seen in the icon of God's image
that appeared on humanity's desktop.

Curiously, God did not choose
maximum modem speed
with which to connect to His world.
Although He had created outer space,
He didn't choose cyberspace
as the means by which
he would highlight his love.
Neither did he download himself
digitized on a 19 inch color monitor.
The incarnation was not virtual reality.
In RealTime the Almighty actually entered
into time and space
through the available port
of a virgin's womb.
Thus, the pace at which
grace came to us
was not instantaneous.
It was the length of time
it typically takes
to grow what love conceives.
And what the Creator conceived
needs no upgrade.
The anti-virus program
is a person who remains the same
yesterday, today and forever.
This Christmas
Jesus the Christ
is just a faith-click away.

Christmas Soldiers of Compassion

Why the Salvation Army deserves our support.

You are soldiers of compassion
on the front lines of despair.
You are armed with love and mercy
with an aim to truly care.

You're a band of brothers, sisters
marching to a different drum,
making music with your service,
giving hope to helpless ones.

You are General Booth's descendents
with a uniform desire
to reach out just like the Savior
to the poor, displaced and tired.

When we go about our shopping,
we can hear the bells you ring.
But as coins clink in your kettles,
God himself begins to sing.

May you sense the Father's presence
as you serve in Jesus' name.
Let the Spirit crown your efforts
though the world denies you fame.

It's Time to Light the Candles of December

Exposing the holiday bandits of envy and greed.

Alas, it's December when darkness prevails.
But also the wonder of Biblical tales.
A miracle oil. A miracle birth.
A miracle visit of One sent to earth.

A season that's marked by tall tapers of wax
that light up our world with the truth they unmask.
This season of Christmas and Hanukah too
means candles for Christians and candles for Jews.
Some grace a menorah and some grace a wreath.
The glow from these candles expose cunning thieves
that lurk in the shadows and hide in the weeds.
One thief's name is Envy. The other is Greed.

These holiday bandits are hungry as sin.
They steal and devour contentment within.
Like vandals they lure us. They're really quite smart.
They pillage and plunder the peace in our hearts.
They kidnap our reason insisting on new
while what we are using is fine and will do.

They hold our minds hostage to where we want more.
More money. More status. More stuff. So much more.
More big screens. More cell phones. More video games.
So much more technology. It is so lame.

These holiday villains just must be exposed.
Their criminal conduct's the cause of our woes.
We're weary. We're listless. We're often depressed.
We're angry. We're in debt. We're way over-stressed.

And all the while famines and earthquakes and war
rob helpless young children of life like before.
No shelter. No supper. No sweet dreams at night.
No hope that injustices will be made right.
No parents. No siblings. No laughter. No time.
No chance for survival beyond eight or nine.

No lie. It's the truth. We are victims you see
of devious Greed and his partner Envy.
They're ruining Christmas and Hanukah too.
But there's a solution. Three things we can do.
The first is to thank God for all that we own.
The second's to care for the needy we've known.
The third is to sponsor poor children abroad.
By sharing with orphans, we're honoring God.

Compassion, World Vision and, yes, World Concern
allow us to reach out to kids who've been burned
by random disasters that leveled their lives
reducing their childhood to hunger and sighs.

It's really amazing. By showing we care,
we'll lock up those bandits that cause our despair.
We'll find renewed freedom from unneeded stuff
and even the courage to shout out "Enough!"

Enough of the shopping. Enough of the crowds.
Enough of more diddlies, for crying out loud.
Enough of just buying for family and friends.
Enough of this nonsense. It's time it all ends.

So as we light candles and ready our homes,
let's welcome the Presence that comes with shalom.
Let's listen for what in our hearts we might hear.
In candlelit silence, we find God. He's here.

In the Bleak Midwinter

The title of a timeless carol describes this time of year.

The reason for this troubling rhyme
is what takes place each Christmastime.
It's eerie. No, it's tragic.
Every year there's something bad.

By Googling you soon will see
December breeds grave tragedies.
Joy to the World is what we sing,
but what we read is sad.

The headlines document our plight.
It's rare that there's a silent night.
The sound of gunshots can be heard.
There're sirens, weeping too.

And Old Man Winter's rarely nice.
His blizzards, floods and storms of ice
result in homelessness and death.
White Christmases turn blue.

In bleak December, airplanes crash,
tsunamis kill and dreams are dashed
by random acts of violence,
depression, suicide.

And when you look at years gone by,
you'll be amazed. You'll want to cry.
In spite of what Christ's birth assures,
we grieve each Christmastide.

NEW YEAR'S EVE

A New Year's Eve Dilemma

At which looking glass to gaze?

Looking in the rear view mirror
is what we tend to do
as we approach each New Years Eve,
the old year finally through.

We glance back at what we achieved,
the things of which we're proud.
We also see what tripped us up
and left us bruised and bowed.

We're prone to look at yesterdays
replaying our regrets.
But such a ploy is foolishness.
It's always a bad bet.

Though rearview mirrors reflect
the past with clear accuracy,
they blind us to what lies ahead.
The windshield lets us see.

So while a backward glance can tempt,
a frontward gaze is best
to face the New Year with its joys,
blind curves, potholes and tests.

SPORTS

BASEBALL

Baseball's Dress Rehearsal

Exploring the uniform thrill of Spring Training.

It's cold up north, but you don't care.
The smell of pine tar's in the air.
The Boys of Summer know it's time.
Spring Training has begun.

You watch them stretch and loosen up
and hear an ump say "batter up!"
The warmth of sunshine melts the blahs
of winter's frigid chill.

Besides the players getting fit,
they'll even sign your youngster's mitt.
It's baseball like it used to be.
Up close and personal.

It is the dream of every fan
to cheer your team and get a tan
while those back home are shov'ling snow
Hey, pass the peanuts please.

And while the games don't really count,
excitement soars and starts to mount.
Spring Training means that op'ning day
is coming into view.

Opening Day is a Day for New Beginnings

Closing the closet door on baseball's skeletons.

Play ball!

After all,
it's opening day.

From behind home plate
a chest-protected umpire
stands erect and
(masking his beaming face)
belts a familiar phrase...

Batter up!

Two words that call an end
to an unbelievably long wait
that has lasted all winter.

But this year
it's not only the batters
whose actions
are dictated by the second
of those two words
that is just two letters long.

Batter UP!

The batters may be up,
but we fans are up too.

We're upset.
We're up in arms.
We're up to speed
on why home run records

have been disappearing
far too fast.

But that isn't all we're up to.
We're fed up, too.
We're fed up with a diet of deception
on which we've been forced to feed
for far too long.
It's enough to make us sick.
And so we are.

We've been duped by buggers
who aren't really the sluggers
they led us to believe they were.

Dopers are more like it.
Performance-enhancing druggies.
Players who've played a game
in pursuit of fame
and in the process
shamed the sport.

Heavens to Murgatroid!
At long last
steroids has been thrown out
attempting to steal the integrity
of America's Pastime.
And all we can say is,
"It's about time!"

Hey batter-batter,
you'd better do more than just
SWING!

In this season of new beginnings.
you'd better do better than that.

Don't just play ball.

Play fair.

Take Me Out to the Ballgame

Why the seventh-inning-stretch song is more than just a song.

Take me out to the ballgame...
Not just any old ballgame.
But a game played
with a horsehide ball.
Horsehide not pigskin.
A hard little white ball.
not a big bouncy brown ball
or a black and white spotted ball.
A game with bases not with hoops
A game with home plate
and not hash marks
A game with catchers not keepers.

Take me out with the crowd...
Not just any old crowd,
but a loud crowd in a classic baseball stadium.
Not a hushed gallery on a manicured golf course
or an elite crowd dressed
to the nines at a purebred track,
but a loud crowd
of every imaginable size and shape
clothed in every imaginable home team apparel.
A loud proud crowd with one thing in common.

They are a family of fans
who feel related to all the brothers
on the field and in the dugout.

Buy me some peanuts and Cracker Jacks...
Not just any old snack will do.
There are certain givens for a game at the yard.
The unshelled salted nuts.
The timeless caramel corn
with a toy surprise in every box.
But don't stop there.
You just gotta have
one of those over-priced hot dogs
served up by those
overweight loud-barking vendors.
A Coke on ice or a beer in hand
is a traditional must to wash down the dust
on a hot summer day
as the wind swirls around the infield.
And don't forget a cup of malted ice cream
with the itty-bitty wooden spoon.
That's a taste treat that will sweeten
even those long bitter days
when your team comes up short.

I don't care if I ever get back...
It's really true.
You wouldn't want to be anywhere else.
The smell of well-oiled ball gloves,
the infield dirt and the grassy outfield
are fragrances that make you wish
time would stand still.
But don't forget your other senses.
Like your hearing for instance.
The piercing crack of a wooden bat
colliding with a 94 mile per hour pitch.

That by itself is enough to raise
goose pimples on your arms.
It's a sound that takes you back
to the days of your youth
when your dad watched you
get your first Little League hit
or when he and your grandpa or (your Uncle Al)
took you to your first Major League game.
It's a sound you could listen to all day.
No wonder they call baseball
our national pastime.
It's a most tantalizing way to pass the time
without being tagged out by guilt.
While a bunted ball rolls slowly
down the third base line,
you feel the stress of work roll off your back.
No wonder we hope for extra innings.
The demands and deadlines of the job can wait.

For it's root, root, root for the home team....
From a solitary "Hey batter, batter"
to a stadium-wide wave,
rooting is as individual as each unique fan's response
or as all-encompassing
as the waving arms on either side of you.
There are chants as old as childhood cheers.
Ones like "Here we go Cubbies. Here we go!"
Or "We want a hit! We want a hit!"
There are choruses of time-honored roots
led by the man at the Wurlitzer organ in the press box.
You know.
Ones like, "Da-duh da duh duh-da. CHARGE!"
And of course there's the age-old Bronx cheer
"#&*@$"

just to annoy the visiting team
in its drab gray traveling uniforms.
Everybody knows that baseball fans
are not allowed to remain silent.
Like the "amens" or "praise the Lords" at church,
the congregation perched above
the hallowed ground of heaven on earth
has a responsibility to raise their voices
and confess their desires
without concern for anonymity.

If they don't win it's a shame....
Whoever said "winning isn't everything"
certainly wasn't a baseball fanatic.
The root word from which the word fan
emerges into the luxury box of linguistics
implies the antithesis of apathy
or a comfort level with loss.
For the true fanatic, defeat is detestable.
The longing for victory is the only thing
that keeps you coming back to the ballpark
game after game, season after season,
century after century
(especially if you are a Chicago Cubs fan).

For it's one, two, three strikes you're out....
Three strikes. Four balls. Nine players.
Three and two. A single. A double. A triple.
A four bagger. A double-play. A triple play.
Three up and three down. A double-header.
Now those are numbers that make sense.
Forget the new math.
The old kind is the only kind that really adds up.
Forget that dreaded report card.
A scorecard is all that really matters.

At the old ballgame...
An old game that is rich
with tradition and historical significance.
An old game that is nonetheless always new.
New players, new uniforms, new ball yards,
new rivalries, new records and new fans.
While it may be an old game, it is a game that,
like a rare vintage wine,
grows better with time.
It improves with age from age to age.
Come autumn time it remains the rage.
This old ballgame can still capture
the imagination of an entire nation
for two weeks every October.
Just listen to the song
the faithful continue to sing
at the top of their lungs
just before the bottom
of the seventh inning.
And as you listen,
look beneath the lyrics
to the mystery they invoke.

A Rose that Grows in Peat

"Reward the player, not the gambler!"
That's the rue and cry.
But let sportswriters beware.
The fragrance in the air
is a bit misleading.
A rose that grows in peat

can't be trusted to stand up straight.
Neither will it last.
It's a plant that lacks integrity
and it's easy to see
it's not the petals
that color the man.
It's the life
from which his petals stem.
In the end it's the full flower
that should be judged,
not just the part we think smells sweet.
A rose by any other name
should be equally scrutinized.
He who is wise knows that
prized varieties don't come cheap.
Their roots go deep.
In Cooperstown (or any town),
an award-winning garden
must be weeded and fenced
lest the beauties on display
simply wilt and fade away.

High Flight

A home run ball reflects on making history
(with apologies to John Magee).

Oh, I was hit by surly Bonds at bat
and danced the skies on tarnished silvered wings.
Sunward I climbed (a much-sought baseball stat),
beyond the wall. A record-breaking thing
of which I long had dreamed. To be that privileged ball
whacked high in the sunlit silence amid fans' frenzied praise.

To be the orb Hank Aaron hoped would stall
and then perchance just melt from solar rays.
But how was I to know the reason why
I topped the windswept heights with easy grace
was rooted in deceit and covered lies?
My dreams for fame became nightmarish pain.
In spite of being claimed by Cooperstown,
my legacy will always be a shame.
The home run ball hit by the steroids clown.

World Series Fever

The present-day draw of our national pastime.

World Series fever.
It's a sickness for which I pray
they will never find a cure.
Its allure is both senseless and sensual.
Hear the sounds of cheering crowds,
home plate umps and sliding into third.
Smell the fresh mown grass
and the oiled leather gloves
(not to mention the unmistakable fragrance
of those stadium vendors' dawgs).
Feel the chill of a cool October night
and the warmth of the bright lights overhead.
Taste the salted nuts and Crackerjacks,
while you watch a game
you first watched with your grampa.
Is it any wonder our national pastime
is enjoyed best in the present tense?
Batter up!

Against the backdrop of applause,
a uniformed ambassador
emerges from a dug-out embassy.
He advances to a diamond-shaped
table of negotiation.
His eyes meet his adversary's.
No words are spoken,
but the interchange has begun.
Snap!
An airborne handful of horsehide
traveling nearly a hundred miles an hour
strikes an awaiting hand gloved by nothing but cowhide.
Stee-rike!
A vocal evaluation
of the placement of said pitch
(announced with dramatic confidence)
meets with the approval of a crouched catcher
but not of a betwixt batter
who shakes his head in disbelief.
Determined to swing next time,
he fails to make contact with the speeding blur of white.
As the third pitch sails outside,
the batter blinks his eyes and cocks his head
but can't believe his ears.
Yeer out!
Without a doubt the man in black
(with the authority of a man of God)
casts a pall of mourning
on the somber congregation.
His unexpected benediction
leaves them suddenly silent with angry grief.
In an attempt to express their sorrow,
the stunned mourners cry out something about
the umpire's need for medical treatment
related to his obvious visual impairment.
But all is not lost.

The cost of victory is about to be paid.
Crack!
A wooden cylinder drills a white stitched ball
deep into right center field.
The cheering fans beyond the ivy-covered wall
watch the wind-swept fly die
beyond the reach of a leaping outfielder
and land in the outstretched hand of a wide-eyed child
(convinced dreams do come true).
Holy cow!
And holy horses too.
You can't help but be grateful for
those sacred barnyard animals
whose lives were sacrificed
in order for their skins to equip a game
that refuses to die
and whose popularity
continues to defy explanation.
Yes!
There's no way to say just why it's so.
It just is. That's all.
Though terror stalks our peace of mind
and nations flirt with war,
when the final score in the fall classic
finds your team on top
all is right with the world.
Seriously…
at least for a week in autumn.

Fall Classic Magic

Analyzing the hypnotic spell the World Series casts.

Crisp fall nights.
Outfield lights.

The "boys of summer" tasting glory
having earned the right.

Horsehide stitch.
Fever pitch.
Those blazing fastballs
warm the evening.
It's an autumn itch.

Hometown fans.
Peanut-littered stands.
With fingers crossed
for no-hit games,
they pray, too, for grand slams.

Pastime now.
"Holy cow!"
These baseball games
in late October
smooth a wrinkled brow.

Men like boys
with pent-up joys.
Their dreams of childhood
left unrealized
in a trunk of toys.

Yet each year,
like a mirror,
each televised
World Series game brings
what"s forgotten near.

FOOTBALL

Worshiping the Pigskin God

Exploring the spirituality of Super Bowl Sunday.

The seats are filled with worshipers.
Their voices chant and cheer.
It's really almost spiritual.
You'd think that God was here.

They raise their hands and close their eyes.
They bow their heads and pray.
What happens next? They genuflect
and then they start to sway.

A wave of praise moves through the crowd.
They stand up to confess
allegiance to the pigskin god
while clad in their team's dress.

Like Romans back in Caesar's time
they watch the sacrifice.
Atonements made on grassy turf
with blood and pain and ice.

And so on this blest holiday
true followers abound.
But church is not the sacred place.
Gridiron's holy ground.

But what of that which matters more
than touchdowns, pads and rings?
Must God be sidelined, sacked or snubbed
for such less noble things?

Can true devotion that we see
this Sunday every year
be matched by what we see in church?
This day's a somber mirror.

BASKETBALL

Cultural Commitment

What March Madness has to do with cultural Christianity.

We hardly watch a game all year
but come World Series time,
we pick a team and place a bet
and sing the "Take Me" rhyme.

At Super Bowl we're instant fans,
but don't ask about teams.
The big game's just a good excuse
to party (so it seems).

The same in March. We all go mad
and watch roundballers score.
A game of hoops we'll take or leave
until the Final Four.

Me thinks I see a pattern here
within our well-honed ways.
We raise the rafters with our cheers
on only certain days.

No wonder many blow-off church,
though they say they believe.
Except for Easter, folks sleep in
until it's Christmas Eve.

Commitment is conditional.
The culture sparks our flame.
We're fans but not fanatical.
Our loyalty's a game.

It's That Time of Year

Looking at March Madness through
the eyes of John Wooden.

John Wooden would what others wouldn't.
Truth be told, the others couldn't

match his record through the years
earned by practice, sweat and tears.

Competition, he'd attest,
fuels the best to stand the test.

That's the reason Coach kept on.
Hope for him was never gone.

Lew Alcindor and Bill Walton
learned the lessons Coach had taught 'em.

Like the fact that discipline
means far more than just a win.

Or the truth that self control
makes a gifted player whole.

There were poems he'd recite
that were fun but never trite.

Faith in Christ, Coach boldly claimed,
shaped the way he coached each game.

Shaped the way he'd build guys up
when they drank from failure's cup.

Shaped the way he helped them see
teamwork leads to victory.

That is why he loves March Madness
with its joy and with its sadness.

And at nearly ninety-six,
Coach still needs his yearly fix.

Waiting for what lies in store,
he will watch the Final Four.

A Wanna-Be Hoopster

Challenging lessons from an autistic high school athlete.

A special needs student,
he dreamed of the day
his coach would say "Jason,
it's your turn to play."

But Jason McElwain
was hardly convinced
his dream would be realized.
He sat on the bench.

While dressed in his street clothes
as managers are,
this wanna-be hoopster
was hardly a star.

He gave the team water.
He handed out towels.
He cheered for his teammates
and protested fouls.

Autistic and awkward,
and often left out,
young Jason refused
to get angry or pout.

He did as requested
and honored his team.
But never gave up
on his unlikely dream.

And then came the last game
and out of the blue
the coach said, "Suit up, son.
Tonight's game's for you."
He sat with his teammates
all beaming with pride.
His team dominated.
Their lead was quite wide.

Just then he heard "Jason,
it's your turn. You're in!

You're part of the team
so go share in our win."
Good Lord, it was magic
as everyone screamed.
This special needs student
was living his dream.

In the space of four minutes,
he scored twenty points.
The grandstands went wild.
Every fan in the joint

knew Jason was gifted.
The whole crowd agreed
that labels are lethal
when you've special needs.

To be called autistic,
you're thought of as odd.
You're misjudged as if you've been
orphaned by God.

How hurtful. How stupid.
How wrong can folks be.
Quite often these kids
are much smarter than we.

From Jason McElwain
we all have been shown...
You can't judge another
by what he's most known.

Within every person
God's image is seen.
So why don't we help them
discover their dreams?

BOSTON MARATHON

Life is Like "The Boston"

There's more to a marathon than meets the eye.

It's a metaphor for living.
Like "The Boston," life's a race.
There are hills, downpours and shin splints.
There's a stiff wind in your face.

While you run it flanked by others,
often times you feel alone.
You get winded and discouraged.
You're exhausted to the bone.

Life is never like a cake walk.
It's a marathon at best.
It's a measure of endurance.
It's a complicated test.

But a second wind awaits you
if you pace yourself each day.
Dropping out is not an option.
Finish strong! Go all the way!

NEWS & POLITICS

Liberty Never Blinks

Reflections on the anniversary of 9/11.

With big sad eyes that never close
she watched those black clouds as they rose
eclipsing New York's brilliant sun
as shadows signaled doom.

Unflinchingly she stared and wept
as towers fell and terror swept
across a city unaware
that held its breath and prayed.

With torch in hand she offered light
to those who searched both day and night
for missing loved ones lost beneath
a mountain of debris.

She stood for hope when hope seemed lost
as rescue workers paid the cost
of burying our broken dreams
that died that dreadful day.

She stood by guarding while we grieved
and heard us say why we believed
that we must seek out terrorists
before they strike again.

And still she stands defiant, strong
unfazed by those who've done us wrong.
And those who try to stare her down
will find she never blinks.

Try to Remember (and Forget)

New lyrics to a Broadway showtune documenting less than Fantastik headlines.

Try to remember
that day in September
when life was changed
for us forever.

Try to recover
a grief that's been covered
by years now past
and prayers unanswered.

Try to replenish
what's slowly diminished.
A faith in God
and love of country...
and honor.

The Big Easy's Hard Year

Reflections on Katrina's Wrath.

Her name was gentle, but that's all.
The day Katrina chose to call,
all Hell broke loose in New Orleans
and Easy became hard.

A YEAR ago she blew through town.
The evidence is still around.
This heartless woman's calling card
has numbers that won't quit.

The cost's in lives and dollars spent
and those who owned but now must rent
plus countless heartache felt by those
whose dreams can't be rebuilt.

New Orleans now is half the size.
What has increased are all the whys
that question how so many still
are homeless and displaced.

O God, please comfort those alone
who have no place to call their home.
And help us all to realize
there's something we can do.

Mother Justice is Blind No More

Right to Life Rulings Challenge Political Correctness.

These are days
to praise our Maker
(and thank our lawmakers).
In a culture
that is speeding
in the direction
of moral retardation,
the right to life
hasn't been completely
left behind.
At least for now,
justice isn't blind
when it comes to

the inalienable privileges
of those partially born
or partially alive.
Eyes closed to truth
have finally opened.
But for how long?
Isn't it about time
Mother Justice's blindfold
be untied for good?
Should parents need a lawyer
just to let their daughter live?
Should a fed-up husband be allowed
to keep his wife from food?
Should a mother
(enveloping a fully-formed baby)
be allowed to refuse delivery
of priority mail at the doorstep
while stamping "return to Sender"
on a love letter from Heaven?

P.S. No matter the hand
that we've been dealt,
life trumps death any day.

A Pain in the Butt

A crude title for a poem about a crude problem.

To do your duty at the pump
is cause for pain within your rump.
It steals your joy and robs you blind
and renders you a grouch.

Yes, getting gas can make you mad,
especially if you drive a Cad.
But even Honda owners cry
to give their car a drink.

The price tag on a barrel of oil
is nothing short of criminal.
It seems, though free, we're hostages
to those who own the crude.

Yet in all things we can give thanks
although it hurts to fill our tanks.
For while, it's true, we pump and weep,
we have the means to pay.

Gas-aholics Anonymous

Acknowledging our dependence is the first of many steps.

Okay let's admit it.
We're gas-aholics.
We crave Saudi oil.
Without it, we're sick.

We guzzle at gas pumps.
We can't get enough.
But feeding our habit
is costly. It's rough.

Our Arab bartender
keeps raising the price.
He knows our addiction,
yet still aids our vice.

With devilish glee
he keeps urging us on
to get fully tanked
till our sanity's gone.

We need to get sober.
We know it. We must.
But who's there to help us.
Just who can we trust?

We drunks need each other.
We can't quit alone.
We don't have the energy
left to our own.

Recovery's essential
through solar or corn.
We must find new sources.
We must be reborn.

So let's take 12 steps
toward the goal to be free
from the bondage of oil.
We must find the key.

The National Daze of Prayer

What's left after the Christian Right prays?

May's first Thursday marks the day
when those inclined take time to pray.
While millions do, far more do not
insisting it's just hype.

"Come on. Get real. A day of prayer?
To live "In God We Trust" is rare.
There is no trust in Washington
and truth is up for grabs."

I hear the cynics in my head.
"If God once lived, He now is dead.
No wonder kids are killed at school
and homelessness won't die."

They're also dazed by what they see.
A camouflaged hypocrisy
where those who claim to speak for God
talk love but walk in hate.

No wonder critics just don't care
about a yearly day of prayer.
And knowing that they feel that way,
we can't just pray but act.

So help me, God. Cause what I do
to challenge what some think of You.
May they in time deny their doubts
and claim You're in control.

Preventing Truth Decay

Exposing the cultural cavity of deception.

Preventing truth decay is tough
when truth portrayed is just a bluff.
The oxymorons in the news
are almost laughable.

Press conferences without the press
are windows dressed without a dress.
They're nothing but hypocrisy.
They're fraudulent. Obscene.

A holy war in Allah's name
can't be as holy as some claim.
It's terrorism birthed in hate.
It's neither just nor fair.

Those prime time programs on TV
are not so prime for families.
There's sex and hard-core violence
that feed our mares of night.

Integrity is often faked,
but such a ploy puts trust at stake.
When what is said is not what is,
corruption wears a crown.

Somehow we've got to tell the truth.
Deception's like a rotten tooth.
Prevention may be difficult,
but it can start with you.

The Price Tag of Being President

Exploring the hidden costs of the office.

The perks of being President
don't really compensate
for all the pressures of the job
and choices that you hate.

You choose to let the nation think
that you are quite inept
because it has no knowledge
of top secrets that are kept.

You choose to live a lonely life
apart from friends back home.
You still care very much for them
but time is not your own.

You choose to let your daughters spend
commencement without you
because you know by showing up
the place would be a zoo.

The price you pay to be in charge
is more than what you make.
Could you have known before you ran
the cost would be so great?

Well if not then, you know it now.
Just maybe that explains
why you're so quick to ask for prayer
and call on Jesus' name.

The Marathon to the White House

The exhausting impact of this presidential race.

The race for the White House is wearing me out.
It's longer than races should be.
I'm losing my interest. Quite honest, I'm bored.
I hate what it's doing to me.

Each morning Tim Russert (with white board in hand)
points out where each runner is now.
It seems they've been running for thirty-six months.
No wonder there's sweat on their brow.

And they will keep sprinting for several weeks more
before some drop out or slow down.
Are these guys on steroids? on Red Bull? Caffeine?
Cross-country they race town to town.

These marathon runners just stop to debate
and then they return to their pace.
I guess their endurance is better than mine.
I'm sick and I'm tired of this race.

Campaigning's a pain in the... Well, you know where.
But can we expect it to change?
Not likely. You kidding? This wild goose chase
is what some (I gander) want. Strange!

About the Author

Greg Asimakoupoulos is the senior pastor of Mercer Island Covenant Church in suburban Seattle. Over the past three decades, he has served congregations in California, Illinois and Washington State. In addition to his weekly preaching ministry, Greg has earned a reputation as a prolific writer. He is the author of ten books and more than three hundred magazine articles. In addition, he has written countless poems about current events and the human experience for numerous websites. He has been a regular contributor to the Partial Observer since 2004.

Greg was raised in Wenatchee, Washington, graduated from Seattle Pacific University and received a Masters of Divinity from North Park Theological Seminary. He and his wife Wendy were married in 1982 and have three daughters.

Made in the USA